GOD KNOWS MY PURPOSE

GOD KNOWS MY PURPOSE

The Life and Legacy of
Rev. Dr. Wealthy L. Mobley SR.
A Man with A Vision

An Authorized Biography
by
Shirley Ann Lott

XULON PRESS

Xulon Press
2301 Lucien Way #415
Maitland, FL 32751
407.339.4217
www.xulonpress.com

Due to the changing nature of the Internet, if there are any web
addresses, links, or URLs included in this manuscript, these may
have been altered and may no longer be accessible. The views and
opinions shared in this book belong solely to the author and do not
necessarily reflect those of the publisher. The publisher therefore
disclaims responsibility for the views or opinions expressed within
the work.

Unless otherwise indicated, Scripture quotations taken from the
King James Version (KJV) – *public domain.*

Paperback ISBN-13: 978-1-6628-2079-3
Hard Cover ISBN-13: 978-1-6628-2885-0

DEDICATION

This book is dedicated to God, the creator of the heavens and the earth, and to Rev. Dr. Wealthy L. Mobley Sr.

God is the author and finisher of my faith. He gave me the courage to put my faith to work in a different way. It was he, who encouraged me to stay in the race. Though, the storm and rain came, strong and mightily. It was Yahweh Shalom, that calmed the raging sea. This, I shall never understand how joy came so speedily. I cannot tell if the storm went right or left. It's still a mystery. I can remember it like yesterday. When I lost my mother, Albirtha Ratliff. He comforted me, with small sips of wisdom, and eyes to see. Thank you Lord, for your grace and mercy.

Although, Rev. Mobley passed away in 2013, this book remained in progress. Reminiscing his life and legacy, it moved me with compassion to complete each chapter for God's glory.

Shirley Ann Lott

TABLE OF CONTENTS

FOREWORD

"The steps of a good man are ordered by the Lord: and he delighteth in his way." (Psalm 37:23)

Walk into your purpose.

Though, we are all made uniquely different, we don't always know what our purpose is, but we are all made purposefully to be used by God. Job positions can be replaced, but people are irreplaceable. Because God has all power, we as people should trust him. *"Trust in the Lord with all thine heart; and lean not unto thine own understanding. In all thy ways acknowledge him, and he shall direct thy paths."* (Proverbs 3:5)

Before meeting Rev. Wealthy L. Mobley Sr., I had served and participated with many ministries and participated in civil rights.

Spirituality is so important in a person's life, that without it, one can often find themselves with emptiness that only God can fill. It is so very important to have God as the centerpiece of your life. Faith and purpose are important to build upon. There are so many obstacles that can sidetrack a person from knowing what their life purpose is.

Your purpose made clear.

I became active in the Civil Rights Movement at an early age. I marched with Dr. Martin Luther King, Jr. in the Summer of 1966, in the highly publicized demonstration for Fair Housing in Marquette Park. From that day forward, I've always felt the need to participate in protests that can help bring about positive change in peoples' lives. Currently, I do actions with an institution called Action Now. There is so much that can be done with community organizations that are aimed towards improvement for social and equal justice. "*I can do all things through Christ which strengtheneth me.*" (Philippians 4:13)

Working and participating in different ministries gave me an opportunity to serve. I believe my true calling is to serve and help others. I began in ministry in the year of 1975. I then organized The Zion Westside Community Church. A church for all people. So many challenges came into my life, but a still voice of strength and hope would always utter in my ear. Now, I know that God will always see me through challenges. I just continue to put my trust in him.

My first encounter with Rev. Mobley was around 2002. It seems so long ago. Rev. Tobey Thornton, a friend and fellow musician stated that he was the musician at a church named Cathedral of Love Missionary Baptist Church on East 75th Street in Chicago. Not knowing then that my future encounter would happen, being that I am a musician and minister.

Faith and Hope are key ingredients in receiving the best that God has for you. Miracles and wonders are on the horizon for those that believe. That's because there is power in God. Everyone must do some self-discovery if they are to reach their fullest potential. Prayer is the door opener.

Later, a friend mentioned that he had established a ministry, and the meetings were being held in a local funeral home on South Halsted Street on Sunday's. While on my way to this meeting, I passed this beautiful church building with a steeple. One particular Sunday, I decided to stop in to be a part of their worship service. Not knowing what to expect in entering, the reception was so cordial. The person that met me at the door identified himself as a deacon of the church, with a big smile. At that point, I introduced myself and was led to the pulpit to sat with the other ministers. I noticed this tall striking figure that was conducting the worship service, who was later introduced to me as Pastor Mobley. After the initial introduction, he asked if I would do the traditional altar call. Through that experience, I became a part of the ministry at The Gospel Truth Missionary Baptist Church.

Because of the relationship that was formed, the writer of this book became a member of this church. Pastor Mobley was a friend and mentor that has inputted into the life of me, and so many others. His life and legacy have been so elegantly portrayed in this book by the author Shirley Lott. So, I recommend this book as a must read.

Your purpose is found in God.

REVEREND WILLIAM T. PITTMAN
Chicago, Illinois
August 24, 2020

ACKNOWLEDGMENTS

I have been blessed to have good people in my life at the right time in support of this book being published. They helped in various ways in it becoming a reality. For this, I would like to offer my gratitude to Reverend Wealthy and Euphemia Mobley, Reverend Elizabeth Taylor, Ruth Webb, Shirley Haynes and Ella Slaughter for the highest level of support in answering the call with materials and guidance to assure that the project moved forward.

Pamille Hudson, my proofreader, for your sharp vision, tireless hands, your interest and patience for the project, and for the level of service you give.

Ann Barnswell, NAACP chairperson, for your words of encouragement and support in the completion of this project.

Evangelist Ruthie Duncan, for your friendship, laughter, and unfailing strength in God to encourage and inspire me and others to walk into God's purpose in life despite your obstacles.

Ricky, De Angelo, and Ricketa, my children, for your support and eagerness to see the book in its completion with the intent that readers will learn from it.

Thank you to The Gospel Truth Missionary Baptist Church family.

The following resources used provided a deeper understanding, and context, and served as a reminder:

Books

Carson, Clayborne, eds. *The Autobiography of Martin Luther King, Jr.* New York: Grand Central Publishing, 2001.

Mobley-Till, Mamie, Christopher Benson, *DEATH of INNOCENCE.* New York: One World, 2003.

References

The World Book Encyclopedia. Vol. 13. Chicago: World Book Childcraft International, 1981.

The World Book Encyclopedia. Vol. 21. Chicago: World Book Childcraft International, 1981

Articles

Davis, Kelsey, "Mound Bayou's history a 'magical kingdom' residents fight to preserve," *Mississippi Today,* May 19, 2018.

Luzenberg, Steve, "The Forgotten Northern Origins of Jim Crow," *Time,* February 12, 2019.

Newer, Rachel, "Mississippi Officially Ratifies Amendment to Ban Slavery, 148 Years Late," *Smithsonian Magazine,* February 20, 2020.

Urofsky, Melvin I., "Jim Crow law," *Britannica,* August 21, 2020.

Newspapers/Periodicals

"Essential pregnancy services agreement reached," *Jackson Advocate*, Vol. 75, 33; May 23, 2013,12A.

Janega, James, "GENNIE MOBLEY JR., CIVIL RIGHTS ACTIVIST," *Chicago Tribune*, March 22, 2000.

Kelvin, Christine A., and Sandra B. Zellmer. "The Flood of 1927." *Mississippi River Tragedies*, 214, 62-78.

Online Sources

Hensley, Erica, "Community health program invests in pregnant women early to disrupt Mississippi's poor birth outcomes," Mississippi Today," March 7, 2020. https://mississippitoday.org/2020/03/07/pilot-community-health-program-disrupts-jacksons-poor-birth-outcomes/

Lester, Connie, "Economic (Labor 1938-2009) Development in the 1930s: Balance Agriculture with Industry." *Mississippi History Now*, 2000-2017. http://mshistorynow.mdah.state.ms.us/articles224/economic-development-in-the-1930s-balance-agriculture-with-industry

U.S. Department of Labor, "History of Federal Minimum Wage Rates Under the Fair Labor Standards Act, 1938-2009," Accessed July 17, 2020. http://www.wagehour.dol.gov

Unpublished

The Gospel Truth Missionary Baptist Church, "*23rd Year Church Anniversary,*" November 9, 2011.

Early Years

"Before I formed thee in the belly I knew thee and before thou camest forth out of the womb I sanctified thee and ordained thee a prophet unto the nation." (Jeremiah 1:5)

It was March 12, 1921 in Minter City, Mississippi that Wealthy Lee Mobley Sr. and his fraternal twin sister Mae Wealthy Mobley were born to Eugene and Elizabeth Mobley.

Mrs. Mobley had both a very devastating and complicated pregnancy with them. Mae was stillborn, and after two more hours of labor, Wealthy was born. He was very sick. The doctor did not expect him to live after his twin sister had died. Wealthy later explained that he believed that God had a divine purpose for his life. For this reason, he lived, and did not die.

Though Wealthy survived his twin sister at birth, he continued to get sick periodically. One hot summer day when he was about 6 years old, he was sick again. He was very weak and could not digest any food. So, his parents sent for the doctor. When the doctor got there, Wealthy could barely hold his head up or stay awake while lying in the bed. The doctor diagnosed him with Sepsis.

Sepsis is a life-threatening blood disease triggered by an infection in a part of the body. For a method of treatment, the doctor told his mother to "put a piece of Days Work Chewing Tobacco in his mouth, and keep him awake, or he would sleep away." So, his mother stayed at his bedside throughout the night praying and comforting him. But, before daylight, Elizabeth fell asleep unexpectedly, and Wealthy woke her up by shaking her saying "momma, momma." When she awoke out of her sleep, she began to praise God by saying "hallelujah" for sparing his life. Wealthy grew stronger as months and days went by. As he grew older, his family gave him the nickname, Sugar Dale.

In 1927, the Delta experienced a great Mississippi River flood, causing thousands of people to relocate because of loss of property and crops. This river flood caused many people to be without a job, food, and shelter. During this time, Wealthy's family moved from Minter City, to his childhood home in Glendora, Mississippi in the region of Alluvial Plain, known as the Mississippi Delta. They lived in a small frame house that had no rooms. He called it a "shotgun house" because the door of the house, had no locks on it. Therefore, you could just push the door open. "Down in the south you used to be able to leave your door unlocked. You can't do that down there now," Wealthy confirms this with a clear conscious. He could not think of anyone who does not have locks on their home doors, even now. Though the house they lived in was small, his mother Elizabeth kept it very clean. When they got settled into their new home Wealthy and his family started to attend church services, Sunday School and Baptist Young People's Union meetings at Saint Mary Church. This church sat on a hill not far from their home. When they went to church, they would take the long way getting there by walking around the hill, rather than climbing it. Only to avoid getting dirty.

Elizabeth was a beautiful tall slender woman with long black hair. Her family called her Liz for short. She was both educated and talented. She attended Louisiana State Normal College in Monroe, Louisiana. Her penmanship was explicit. For example, she would send a note up town to the store. They would ask who wrote the note because it was written so well. Also, she wrote speeches for her children to say at church on Easter Sunday. Not only was she a good writer, she would get the Sears Catalogs and make her children's clothing such as, knickerbockers. She was very active in the church as a musician. She played the organ for the church and sang gospel solos. She had a beautiful singing voice. She would sometimes just sing throughout the house while either washing or cooking. When Wealthy became older, he realized that his singing abilities came from listening to his mother sing.

It was amazing to Wealthy how his mother and grandmother, Mary Smith would enjoy church. This he did not understand as a child. While they were inside the church shouting and praising God, he and his siblings, Eugene Jr. and Hosea would sometimes go outside the church to play with one another. Every Sunday after the church service ended, the church members would sit outside the church at tables covered with white sheets, used as tablecloths and had dinner together as a family.

After moving to Glendora, Mississippi, Wealthy's father became a sharecropper. Everyone called him and Eugene Jr., Gene for short. The occupation of a sharecropper came into existence less than a century after slavery. It consisted of hard domestic work, picking cotton, chopping wood and plowing the fields. While working, his body would be drenched in sweat from the hot glistening sun.

His parents would grow their own vegetables and fruit trees. Eugene Sr. would raise and kill his own hogs and cows. He would hang them up, take the melt from the animals and put it on the coals of the fire and cook them. For extra money, he would cut hair when he could. As a child, Wealthy did not feel his family was living in depression because they had plenty of food. But looking back over his life as an adult, his family did live in poverty. But, because of the love his parents had for him and his siblings, this was blinded.

At about 8 years old, Wealthy began to do chores. His chores were to pick cotton, clean the barn, throw hay, feed the chickens, and bring the mule and cows out daily. One day, he hooked a horse to a stalk cutter and started to cut stalk. At such a young age, he could have fallen off either seriously hurting or killing himself. But this did not frighten Wealthy. He would work all day long with no shoes on his feet. When he came home after working out in the field all day, his feet would be scorching hot from the dirt in the field. He would look for a cool spot on the porch for them, but his mother was one step ahead of him. She would have a tub of water on the porch to bathe him. Wealthy remembered staying on the porch to dry off from the sun. While Wealthy was drying off on the porch, his mother would be preparing a typical meal of salt pork, tomato gravy and rice. Wealthy suggests that this small meal would have "you licking your fingers."

Wealthy remembered his family having a fish fry every Saturday evening with freshly made lemonade. In his opinion, that was some of the best tasting lemonade that had ever been made. His grandmother Mary Smith, his father, and other men would get their nets, go out into the lake, put their nets down and come back with a lot of fish. While some of the men were cleaning the fish, others would fill a big black pot with grease and fry it. One Saturday, his father caught a very large ghoul fish. His mother took it out of its tough skin, cut it up, and made some tomato gravy with it. One other Saturday fish fry, his aunt Lucille Randall, whom was a school teacher in Greenwood, Mississippi, brought a big buffalo fish and fried it. Occasionally, his uncles would play a game of softball. He would be the pigtail. But he was so excited about it. He looked forward to being a part of the game every chance he could. Wealthy's family enjoyed sharing and spending time with one another.

Living in the Great Depression (1929-1939)

"But my God shall supply all your need according to his riches in glory by Christ Jesus."
(Philippians 4:19)

I n the early 1930's, Wealthy's father fell on hard times as a sharecropper. He had worked all year long growing crops. But at the end of the year, he came out in the hole, according to the boss. But he was not being truthful with Eugene Sr. He wasn't going to tell him that farm annual income dropped from $287 to $117. He did not feel obligated to tell him anything. Because of economic reasons, the boss really was the one in the hole. So, Wealthy's father had to work harder for the financial loss and price difference. When this happened, Eugene Sr. didn't say anything. Wealthy implies, "it was best that he did not."

Yes, the bossman did get away with this scheme, because black people in the south during this time didn't have a voice, nor much of an education. Though slavery in the United States was abolished in December 1865, black people were still being beaten and lynched in the Mississippi Delta as if it still existed.

There were 27 of the 36 states that submitted their paperwork to ratify the Thirteenth Amendment that abolished slavery in 1865. Mississippi was not one of the states that favored it at that time. Later, Mississippi submitted their required documents to ratify the Thirteenth Amendment in 1995, but they missed one critical step. That step was to notify the U.S. archivist concerning their late decision. So, two residents found the error February, 2013, contacted their state, and explained the mistake. Now, Mississippi has officially satisfied all requirements to ratify the Thirteenth Amendment to abolish slavery.

The color of black people's skin did define how white people should treat them in respect to the Jim Crow Laws. The bill for the Jim Crow Laws passed around 1877. This occurred about twelve years after slavery was abolished. It's obvious, the Jim Crow Laws were created as a form of retaliation for slavery getting abolished. Black people were dehumanized to feel that they were less than any other race just for being black. These laws gave white people the right to continue with scapegoating and oppressing black people. It was not created fairly to judge black people by the content of their character, but by their skin color. But, some things did not change. During this time, the white people still wanted black women to cook, clean, and take care of their children.

Eugene Sr.'s boss let him know he was in the hole. So, Wealthy's father invested money he had on hand to gambling. He had hoped to win more money with that, to support his family. Sadly, this did not happen. He lost all of the money he had left. So, when Christmas came, Wealthy and his siblings looked in their stockings, and nothing was in them. This was very disappointing to Wealthy. Because every year for Christmas they would get apples, oranges, and candy in their stockings. With a low calm voice he acknowledges, "that hurt me. But anyway, the Lord has made up with that so many, many times over."

A major decrease in their food supply occurred because they didn't have any money. Wealthy's mother didn't have any meat to cook for Sunday's dinner. So, while walking to church, his mother spoke a word of faith saying, "boy the Lord is going to provide for us." So, on their way back home from church, there was a duck that had been winged. He and his brothers caught the duck and screamed out with joy saying, " momma, momma, momma" while Wealthy holding the duck up in his hand. He recalls how his mother "just fell down with them, on her knees like a hen that loved her chickens, gave thanks to God, and cooked it for dinner."

Later, Eugene Sr. sectioned off the back of the house to allow an attractive bright skinned lady by the name of Rosa Lee to board there. This lady worked in a hotel for men. One evening she did not show up for work. So, some white men came from the hotel and knocked on the door extremely hard. Liz answered, "who is it?" The men said, "open this dame door." She apparently didn't open the door as fast as the men would have liked, so they took it upon themselves and shot the door opened. Wealthy thought when they had shot the door opened, that the men had shot his mother. The men entered the house shouting "where is Rose?" Liz said, "sir, I don't know where she is." Then they asked, "where is Gene?" She replied pleasantly, "I don't know where he is." Before leaving, they took some kerosene and threw it in their wood burning stove and blew it up. That scared Wealthy. He thought the men were going to kill them. Wealthy predicts, "they could have killed us and nothing would have been done about it. In this time, they would hang a white man for stealing a horse; but wouldn't bother him for killing a black person."

Blacks had very few rights living in the Mississippi Delta because of racial discrimination. Some of the disadvantages Wealthy remembered living in the south were the signs hanging up, referencing two different water fountains. One sign hanging had colored and another had white. Black and white people were not allowed to drink from the same water fountain. He remembered that black people could go to the show, but not allowed to sit near white people. They would have to sit in the balcony of the movie theater. Because of these systematic depressions against black people, Wealthy's parents did not let him go to the show. This he did not miss because they did not have a television at the time. But they did have a radio to listen to as a source of getting news and entertainment.

Not long after a mob of white men broke into their home, Wealthy and his family moved to Tutwiler, Mississippi. While in the process of enrolling him into Rosenwall Elementary School, it was strange to Wealthy that the birth records, had him listed as the still born, and his twin sister Mae as the surviving child. His parents had to get the birth records fixed before he could start school. Eventually, his birth records were fixed and he began going to school 4 months out of a year. He and his siblings walked about 4 miles to get there. When Wealthy did attend school, it was like going on vacation. He worked out in the field more than he went to school. So, whenever he went to school, he was excited about it. One day, while Wealthy was on his way to school, between his grandmother's house and their house, there was a little log that he'd usually cross over the creek on going to school. He stepped on the log to cross the creek, and a black snake jumped high up from underneath the log and tried to bite his hand. Wealthy moved his hand quickly. This is something he has never forgot after becoming an adult.

A Great Burden

When Wealthy was 12 years old, his mother had taken sick while being pregnant. The number of months pregnant is unknown. So, his grandmother began to come over and help take care of her daughter and assure that her grandchildren had food to eat. Elizabeth continued to get worse. She had gotten so sick that she could no longer take care of her youngest son Leroy, so she wrote a letter to her sister Lucille, asking that she come and get him. Her sister came to get him, and raised him as her own child, changing his name to Leroy Randall.

In the Mississippi Delta, black women were not getting the prenatal care that women are getting today. During this time, there were very few, doctors, and hospitals in the Delta. So, Mississippi had midwives to help women give birth in the comfort of their own homes. Now, the Mississippi State Department of Health has approved women who have been deemed to have low-income, and a high-risked pregnancy to be eligible for Perinatal High-Risk Management. Some of the programs consists of health education, and nutritional guidance.

In March 1933, Elizabeth and her unborn twin boys died before she could give birth to them. Wealthy was heartbroken from the death of his mother. He remembered a boy that went to the same school as he, and how a couple of weeks earlier, his mother had passed. He wondered within himself how it felt for the young man to lose his mother. Then, just a couple of weeks later, his mother passed. With tears in Wealthy's eyes, he states, "I missed her, and I still do, because she was such a wonderful lady." He gives thanks to God for the 12 years he had her in his life.

Not long after Wealthy's mother passed. His father abandoned him, Eugene Jr. and Hosea. Causing them to move in with their grandmother Mary. She was a single parent. Her husband Frank had passed when Wealthy was about 2 years old. But she did not hesitate for one moment to take her grandchildren in and raise them as her own. Wealthy missed his mother dearly, but because of the love his grandmother had for him and his brothers, that helped him through it.

Though, Wealthy was very thin yet tall, he worked very hard out in the field. He would usually pick 200 pounds of cotton a day. He worked out in the field daily, unless it either rained or he had school. One afternoon, while Wealthy was doing some work outside around the house, a Caucasian man came and asked Wealthy "where is your daddy?" He explained that he didn't know where he was. So, the man told him, "I want you to come over here and get this mule and go to plowing." Wealthy responded, "yes sir." Then he watched the white man until he got out of his sight. Then he took off running to his grandmother. The next morning that same man came and asked Mary "where that boy at?" In a stern voice she said, "sir, this boy didn't make no contract with you, his father did. I don't think you need to come over here bothering him." Wealthy was peaking behind the curtains from inside their house during their discussion. She was a very brave woman. The white man could have killed her, and nothing would have been done about it.

One other day, Mary told Wealthy to go and get the cow. He mumbled under his breath saying, "go and get it yourself." She did not ask him twice. Wealthy went to bed at about 9:00 PM that night. He was sleeping good on his feather mattress. At about 10:00 PM, Mary got a singer sewing machine cord and whipped him so until his long sleeping gown went up to his waist. As he was getting the whipping, his grandmother was repeating what he had said earlier that day, "GO AND GET THE COW YOURSELF." He gives thanks to God for that whipping. He felt it helped to steer him in the right direction in life. He never disrespected his grandmother again from that night forward. He learned to embrace the love and knowledge that she had to give for his good.

The Bright Lights

Two years later, after the death of her daughter Elizabeth, Mary thought it would be better to move to Chicago, Illinois. She felt Chicago had better resources than Mississippi did for her family. Before Wealthy and his siblings were informed of anything, his Cousin Johnny Green had come to Tutwiler, Mississippi to pick them up in what Wealthy described as an "old opened taxi." He and his family packed their things inside an opened air cab. They had so much packed inside the air cab that they had to tie two hogs on each fender, and a sewing machine on the top of it. While on the way to Chicago, it began to snow. By the time they had gotten to Memphis, Tennessee, the left side of Jonny's face was filled with snow, it was snowing so hard. This was the first time Wealthy had seen bright lights that night. He was mesmerized by the bright lights. He said within himself, "I heard of Chicago. I was wondering would it be the same, like it is in Mississippi. We are used to picking cotton, doing our chores, going to get the cow." They then crossed the bridge into Blytheville, Arkansas. The streets were full of snow. As Johnny was driving, there was a white man driving in the middle of the road with a white woman in the passenger seat. Instead of them getting over, for Johnny to pass, he stayed in the middle of the road, and Johnny didn't move over either. So, the white man ended up swerving into a ditch. Wealthy's family did not hesitate to get out of their car, and help the white man get back onto the road.

Thereafter, slowly driving in slippery snow, they made it to Chicago safely on December 25, 1935. However, Mary and Wealthy's older brother Vernon Brown came in 1937.

Nevertheless, Wealthy, Eugene Jr., and Hosea, lived with his aunt Lucille, and her family. They lived in a 3 or 4 bedroom home on the 2900 block of South Vernon Street. Wealthy was still in awe with the bright lights of Chicago only because they didn't have any street lights while living in Mississippi. When it got dark in the south, a person could barely see their hand. But in the city of Chicago, Wealthy could see and hear many cars as they drove pass his home during the night. This was a different life for Wealthy, but he managed to adapt.

After settling into their new home, Wealthy's Aunt Lucille enrolled him into Doolittle Elementary School. He started out being in the 5th grade. Wealthy was aware that at 14 years old, he should have been in high school. Because of Wealthy's age, and meeting the school expectations academically, he was later moved to the 8th grade. Wealthy implied that the learning he had gotten from Rosenwall Elementary School in Tutwiler, Mississippi was equivalent to that of high school in Chicago. This did not discourage Wealthy at all. He enjoyed going to school as well as learning. In this school, he became more involved by going on field trips. He remembered specifically going to the Field Museum and going to different parks. He also came to know Sam Cooke and his brothers, Bill, L. C., and Charles at Doolittle Elementary School. Wealthy remembered he and Bill, Sam's oldest brother, being in the same classroom at the school. They became good friends, and Wealthy begin to hangout at the Cooke's residence. Wealthy adds, "I've ate many meals at the Cooke's house between the late 30's and early 40's."

In the late 1930's, Wealthy attended Dunbar High School. He did well academically in this school as well. He was a quick learner. His favorite subjects were reading and math, specifically fractions. In this school he began getting more involved socially. He volunteered to become a crossing guard because he enjoyed being a leader and helping others. He also enjoyed sports. At the age of 17, after school, he would go to get coal from the train and sell it for $.25 a basket so that he could go to the school ball games. He did not participate in these activities at the Rosenwall school in the south. The only thing that he did there was his academic studies. So, he found that it was resourceful, and exciting to attend these things at Dunbar.

Wealthy went to school consistently from the ages of 14 and 17 years old. Later, his education was interrupted by a program originated by President Roosevelt in 1935 called the Work Progress Administration. This program was a national work program designed to provide relief, by employing millions of people during the Great Depression. Being that Wealthy was the oldest sibling in the house at the time, he either had to be on work relief, or go back to live in Mississippi. Wealthy believed that they wanted to send him back. But an African American man named Mr. King advocated for Wealthy. He remembered this man to be somewhat of an activist. He spoke on Wealthy's behalf concerning a need to be on work relief. Wealthy stayed 3 days and 3 nights at the relief station eating bologna and drinking water. Mary stayed right there with him until he got on work relief. Even though, Wealthy went through this process of inequality, he believed that God was preparing him for his purpose in life.

After Wealthy got on work relief, he started working for Heinman Cottage Poultry driving a truck, delivering eggs and chicken through WPA. He met some encouraging and helpful white and black men while on this job. Some of the men were old enough to be his father or grandfather.

Wealthy believed that he was getting experience from these men.

At one time, Wealthy began to get kind of bitter about the WPA taking him out of school. He could not understand why they would take him out of school like they did. He felt he needed to be in school learning. Nevertheless, he continued to go to work because he didn't want to be forced to return to Mississippi. So, he was working every day for a flat fee of $27 a month. "During this time, this was a lot of money," he explained. But it was not enough for food to last the whole month. To get by, his grandmother would send his siblings to get commodities, fruits, and vegetables from a nearby food pantry in their community.

BECOMING A MAN

"When I was a child, I spoke as a child, I understood as a child, I thought as a child: but when I became a man, I put away childish things." (1 Corinthians 13:11)

B eing that Wealthy had been working since the age of 8 years old, working had become a form of relaxation to him. So, he could not find time to date. He remembered beautiful girls used to come to their house and help his grandmother wash. Wealthy knew that the girls that came over to his house had an interest in him. But when they would come over, he would leave. It wasn't that he didn't like girls, but he just was not ready to date. I told my grandmother, "I ain't never going no place. I'm staying right here with you." Mary told Vernon to start taking him out so that he could meet some girls. When he took Wealthy out, girls would just be all around him. "I would say to myself, why don't y'all just get away, get away, get away," said Wealthy.

He began to come out of his shyness. Then, he started going to parties with a friend from work named Arthur Adams. But finally, one young lady got his attention. Her name was Essie Reed.

Wealthy began to make time for Essie to go on dates. They went to the movies, plays, ice shows and ball games. They enjoyed doing these things together. Finally, they fell in love and decided that they would get married. Wealthy was 19 years old at the time, and Essie was 17 years old. Wealthy's dad and Essie's mother went down to the city hall with them, because they were not old enough to get a marriage license in Chicago, IL. After getting married they conceived a baby girl in 1942. Wealthy named her Phyllis.

God Provides

Within the same year, Wealthy's job at Heinman Cottage Poultry had folded. Being that Wealthy was already a provider, he knew he needed a job to support his family. So, one morning at 10:00 am, He said, "the Spirit told me to go back to Swift." He had previously been going there looking for work. He had one quarter in his pocket. Back then the speed car rides were only $0.07. When Wealthy got to Swift,

the room was full of men. A man was standing on a platform. When Wealthy walked up, he couldn't even get in
there. Wealthy insist that, "all I could do was stand in the
door." The man on the platform said, "hey you!" Everyone
started looking back. Wealthy responds, "you mean me!"
He replied, "yeah! You want a job?" Immediately, without
hesitation Wealthy says, "yeah, man I want a job!" He
adds, "come on out here then!" From that day, Wealthy
began working for Swift Company delivering packages.
He believed that if he had not obeyed the Spirit, things
wouldn't have worked out that way. Not even a year of being
at this job, Wealthy was notified by letter that he had been
inducted into the US Army.

WORLD WAR II 1942-1945

"A time to love, and a time to hate, a time of war and a time of peace." (Ecclesiastes 3:8)

It was December 1941 that the United States declared war after the American naval base at Pearl Harbor went under attack by the Japanese naval task force. The following year, Wealthy was notified by letter that he had been drafted into the US Army. This letter specified the date in which he should go take his physical examination located in downtown Chicago.

Wealthy was diagnosed with a small hemorrhoid problem. This did not stop the US Army draft process for him. He later received another letter explaining that he had met the army's physical standards. He was then inducted into the US Army December 27, 1942. After he was inducted into the army, he had the hemorrhoids surgically removed.

Of course, this letter did not tell him that he would later become a legendary of his own time for being part of a legacy, such as World War II.

Although he was going to a place he had never been before, he was not afraid. He just simply said within himself, "this is where I live, and I am going to fight for my country." His wife wanted him to stay with her and the baby. That is a normal impulse for a wife who loves her husband, but Wealthy knew he couldn't stay. He began to prepare himself for a new chapter in his life. Before he left to begin his life experiences in the army, Wealthy spoke to his grandmother, Anna Mobley, on the phone about being inducted into the US Army. She responds to him, "we're praying for you, because they are taking men from down here too." Another thing she told him, "don't you volunteer for nothing, but do whatever they tell you to do." Looking back over his life at the age of 91, he knows that it was mandated by God that he should go. It was for his learning and prepared him for pastoring in times such as these.

Boot Camp Training

First, Wealthy went to Camp Fort Custard, MI. He underwent intense physical training and land navigation in the dark. He had to get up at about 5:00 am to do drills. He trained to operate the rifle in the dark. After completing training to shoot an M1 rifle, he received a medal for sharp shooting. However, Wealthy learned how to shoot while living in Mississippi. He had to carry the M1 rifle that weighed 10 pounds and shovels and other things and walk for about 10 miles. Also, he was trained to peel potatoes, serve, wash dishes, and clean-up around the area. All this was to train him to be part of the team.

Second, he went to Camp Fort Grant, IL., a training center for additional basic training. He worked in the bakery. He was trained to bake bread. While in training in Illinois, Wealthy took furlough to spend time with his family on weekends.

Third, he went to Camp Fort McCoy, WI., for camouflage school. He learned to crawl on his knees with his camouflage garments and blend in with nature. Also, he was taken up into an airplane to identify what he could see from a high distance.

Fourth, in 1944, Wealthy went to Camp Ellis, of Illinois for more camouflage training to prepare to go overseas. He had to crawl on the ground and under barbwire. If he had not followed through with all training, he would have been imprisoned. He explained that in training, it was programmed in him that he had to like it. So, he really started to like being in the army so much that he was going to reenlist, but he thought about what his grandmother said, "don't volunteer to do nothing." After completing all these trainings, he rose in ranks from Private First Class to Buck Sergeant. He then decided to get a few days furlough to go home with his family again before boarding a train to go to New York.

From New York, he boarded a ship to Marseille, France, an independent country of Europe. Then he was stationed as a Sergeant in Rennes, France where his assignment in the 9th Air Core began. He was responsible for ordering supplies such as gas, food and clothing. whatever the soldiers needed. Wealthy remembered that whenever he would place an order, the same delivery service he once worked for, Swift would make the deliveries.

Army Segregation

After Being on base a few weeks, Wealthy noticed that the US Army was segregated. The white soldiers were on one side of town, and the black soldiers were on another side of town. They were not allowed to go in the area where the white soldiers were unless they were delivering supplies to them. Though Wealthy had the rank of a sergeant, he did not have any white soldiers under his command. The African American soldiers that were under his command were old enough to be his father. One day Wealthy asked a question. "Lord why you got me here?" He did not get an answer right away. But as the wisdom of God increased in his life, he is now convinced that it was for his purpose in God.

Since Wealthy was stationed close to Paris, he and other soldiers would get weekend passes and go to Paris, Left Bank, Right Bank and the Seine River for relaxation. The first subway that Wealthy had ever been on was in the beautiful city of Paris, France. He loved the view of Paris from the subway. Going there was a way for him and the other soldiers to get away from it all and enjoy themselves.

When Wealthy went to Cherbourg, Germany, he found out that Caucasians had spread rumors that the Black people were part monkey. As he and other soldiers were walking, little children came and asked to see their monkey tails. Wealthy told the children to, "get away from here." But when the white women found out what the black men had, the white men didn't have a chance. One day Wealthy and some other black soldiers were out at a bar, the white men began to wonder why the women were going to the black men. I told them, "because you came over here and lied, telling people that black people have tails." After speaking out against scientific racism, Wealthy drove a motorcycle to the city of Frankfurt, Germany and then enjoyed a night out in Paris.

Segregation in the US Army continued until this breakthrough, Lieutenant General George Patton, who told Wealthy, "send me some soldiers." Wealthy said, "we only have the blacks," and the Lieutenant said, "I didn't ask you about no color." Wealthy did as the Lieutenant had commanded him. That is when things began to turn around for blacks. When the US Army began to allow blacks to fight in the war. The blacks and whites became integrated.

Wealthy L. Mobley, Sr. in the US Army

War Stories

One day, Wealthy was driving a supply truck on the road of France. In comparison, the two-way roads there were as wide as an alley in Chicago. He was taking a load of gasoline to the line alone. While going down a hill, he tried slowing the pace of the truck and found that the breaks had gone out. The road was very rough and steep. This really scared him. He knew that if the truck crashed, the gasoline could cause an explosion and kill him. He didn't know anything else to do other than pray. So, he closed his eyes, praying "Well Lord, I'm in your hands." The natural man in Wealthy just knew his life would end that moment. But, after he prayed, the truck stopped in a nearby village crashing into nothing. This caused a faith increase in God for him.

Wealthy remembers taking another load of gasoline to the line in Cherbourg, Germany. When he got there, they were fighting with the German soldiers. When the captain saw Wealthy there in the midst of the fighting, he demanded the soldiers to get him out of there. "They turned me around. But what had happened was, one of the German planes came down on me. I could just here the bullets coming down towards me sounding like a machine gun," said Wealthy. But, every one of the bullets missed him. After the fighting was over, Wealthy saw the soldiers' lifeless bodies stacked-up like coal wood.

Wealthy, as Staff Sergeant was stationed overseas in Cologne, Germany. Their assignment for that day was to build a bridge that would extend across the Rhine river. They had worked on the bridge all day long. After the bridge was completed, a friend of Wealthy's named A.J. Spencer, a jeep driver, had taken one of the captains across it. But on his way back, the Germans had planted a mine under the bridge. The mine blew him to pieces. He reminisced his death saying, "the way he died stayed with me for many years before getting over it."

There was a German woman who had been raped. She was escorted by police to the base where the black soldiers resided in Germany. She had told the police that a black soldier had raped her. Wealthy remembered this humiliating moment in detail like yesterday, "they called us all out to line up, even myself. It was about forty men that was in my platoon." The woman was to go down the line to see if she could pick the man that had raped her. Without a bitter attitude he says, "I could remember that woman walking slowly down the line of army men to observe each man." When the woman got to Wealthy, she stood in front of him for about an hour. Wealthy neither said a mumbling word, nor did he get out of his salute position. After the lady stood in front of Wealthy all that time, saying nothing, but just staring at him. She finally walked further down and picked the man that allegedly raped her. To Wealthy's understanding, her accuser was lynched like they did black men in the South.

The Germans broke through the line and scattered the US Seventh Army. Over a hundred or so men scattered going different ways. Some got killed and some got away. Wealthy ended up all the way in the country of Belgium to be reassigned. He was assigned to the British Army for about a month with the Red Ball Express. The plan was to stay with the Red Ball Express until they got ready to go to Japan. But before they could go to Japan, World War II had ended September 2, 1945. Their assignment in Japan was canceled and so instead they boarded a ship to go to New York. A few months later, Wealthy was honorably discharged from the US Army in December, 1945.

When Wealthy came home from the US Army his family was happy to see him. They all were happy that he made it out of the army without being seriously injured or even killed. Countless civilians and military died in World War

II. They had a lot to be thankful for. His daughter Phyllis was three years old and didn't know who he was when he came home from the army. But, it didn't take long for them to build a relationship. She later became a daddy's girl. A few years later, Wealthy and his wife conceived a son in 1947 naming him, Wealthy Lee Mobley, Jr.

As the years went by, Wealthy and Essie became distant in their love for one another, and later divorced. Wealthy believes that being away in the US Army for 3 years caused their separation. Essie was young with a child, without her husband, explained Wealthy. This alone caused her to be lonely. During the time when he was in the army, wives were not allowed to live on base with their spouse. Some years later, this changed. Soldiers are now able to reside on the base with their wives.

WORK WHILE IT IS DAY

"Whatsoever thy hand findeth to do, do it with thy might; for there is no work, nor device, nor knowledge, nor wisdom, in the grave, wither thou goest." (Ecclesiastes 9:10)

Wealthy was employed with Ford Motor Company in September 1950 as a Skilled Laborer. His starting salary was $1.05 an hour. During this time, this hourly wage was a lot due to the cost of living. Because the minimum hourly wage was $0.75 in the state of Illinois. Then it increased to $1.00 in 1956. With the pay Wealthy was getting, he was able to manage his money well while providing for his family. When he worked overtime, he brought home between $150.00 and $200.00 every 2 weeks. For example, he would fill his freezer with meats for $20.00 that lasted for a month. Also, he paid rent at $60.00 a month. He had a little money to put away inside the credit union. He brought his cars from these funds.

In 1951, Wealthy was laid off from the Ford Motor Company. He got a job at Ford City Manufacturing in the maintenance department making about $2.00 an hour. After working there for a year, he got a letter from Ford inviting him to come back. Wealthy heard in the Spirit, "go back." So, he left a job that was paying twice as much as Ford. He didn't question the Spirit, he just did it. Looking back over his decision there was no regrets, and in 1959 that company dissolved.

Ford Motor Company was well known for selling its affordable vehicles. Wealthy worked as a Skilled Laborer for 8 years. For the first two years, he was unloading box cars. The next six years he was put on the line installing the windshield wipers on the vehicles. Wealthy took pride in working for a company such as this. Sometimes when he would be out and about, he would see a new car on the road made by Ford. He was happy to acknowledge that he took part in building the vehicle one way or another.

Racial Discrimination

Although, Wealthy loved working at Ford Motor Company, he had some difficult times there. One day, Wealthy started working at 3:00 PM. A Caucasian foreman named Mike said to Wealthy, and some other laborers, "Fellows I want you to unload this car. When you're through with it, take it easy." Then another car came in, and the foreman said, "You guys are going to have to do that one." Wealthy and the other workers said, "what?" They replied to the foreman 'what' because he hadn't told the white guys to do anything the whole time. They were over there laughing about it. Wealthy didn't mind working, but he didn't appreciate the foreman undermining his intelligence. In his opinion, that's what the foreman was doing. It really bothered him that they were being told to do all this work, and the white guys hadn't done a thing the whole evening. By this time, it was between 8:30 pm and 9:00 pm; then another car pulled in there. "I got so mad," Wealthy explained. Wealthy began to react to his emotions. So, Wealthy saw a crowbar and picked it up. He was going to hit the foreman with it but a friend of his named James grabbed the crowbar, taking it out of Wealthy's hand saying "NO, NO." Wealthy is thankful to God for James for stopping him from physically assaulting the foreman. He said, "I shall never forget it. Lord, I thank you." This was the only event to occur that caused him to get so angry.

One day, Wealthy was sent home from work with no given reason, though overtime was available. After he left, they allowed a Caucasian man to work in his position with less seniority. The union found out about it, and Wealthy got paid for it.

These, events did not change the love Wealthy had for his job. He feels that working with people and being obedient was a part of his spirituality. He took pride in the work he did. When they gave him a job to do, he did it. He did his job when they were looking and when they were not. When they would leave and come back, they would see what a good job he had done and say, "job well done Moe." That's what they called him at the job.

After eight years of working at Ford Motor Company as a Skilled Laborer, Wealthy was promoted to Semi-Skilled Lift Truck Driver, unloading boxcars. Wealthy became one of the best lift truck drivers at Ford. He was so good at his job, the foreman would call Wealthy at his home, and at church asking him if he could come to work. Being that Wealthy was so loyal to his job he would go to work on his off day. For example, on a Sunday afternoon, Wealthy was singing in the choir. Someone from his job called the Original Mount Pleasant Missionary Baptist Church asking him can he come to work. Wealthy's response was "yes". So, Wealthy went straight to work after leaving church. He would work from Sunday Mid-Noon until Monday night. His wife Euphemia would send his dinner by his brother Eugene Jr.

At one time Wealthy had a desire to become a foreman at the Ford Motor Company. But after observing how the foremen were being disrespected verbally, he withdrew his application. He felt he could not handle being talked to as if he were less than a man. Also, because he loves people, he did not want to take part in degrading another man. Wealthy remembered seeing three Caucasian men that had hung themselves on the worksite. One was found on the dock, another on the chassis line, and the third one was found on the frame line. One of which was a foreman, and the other two were laborers. Wealthy believed that these men committed suicide because they were intimidated by other employees.

'Job Well Done'

Wealthy retired from Ford Motor Company in October 1980 as a Semi-Skilled Lift Truck Driver making $8.13 an hour. He worked for this company for 30 years. Though he retired from the company, he still felt he was a part of it because: (1) He still got an employee discount on the purchase of a vehicle. (2) He got a letter when they get ready to vote on contracts. (3) Every year after he retired he got a bonus.

EUPHEMIA

"Whosoever findeth a wife findeth a good thing, and obtaineth favour of the Lord."
(Proverb 18:22)

E uphemia was born in a small town called Omaha, Nebraska, November 1, 1920 to John Hugh and Willie Densley-Haynes. She graduated from Tech High School within her community. She had two children from a previous marriage, Donald and Barbara.

It was in Chicago, that Wealthy met and fell in love with the attractive and loyal Euphemia, whose humor would grace a room. When she saw Wealthy for the very first time in December 1950, she was instantly attracted to him. Some people may call this love at first sight.

Euphemia came to know Wealthy by her living with his Aunt Lucille. His aunt had a club called the Louisiana Club. This club was for women. All the women that were members, were from Louisiana. Wealthy was a sweetheart of this club.

He would just bring the ladies to the club and take them back home. One particular time, Lucille held a meeting in her home for the club members. Wealthy brought the club members to her house. His aunt owned a two-flat building at the time. While the meeting was going on, Euphemia stood on the top step watching Wealthy's interactions with these women. She admired how respectful and kind he was to them. After the meeting, she asked Lucille about him. Later, Lucille introduced them to one another. From that day forward, they began going on dates spending quality time with one another. They both had just come out of a failed marriage and did not want to go through another no time soon. Therefore, they had lots to talk about.

They enjoyed spending time with each other so much that they became roommates. She and Wealthy shared a hobby for fishing and traveling. Euphemia was so good at fishing, that she taught Wealthy how to cast his fishing rod. "She was a fisherman," he commented. This time spent with one another, was enjoyable. There were times just out of the blue, Wealthy would say, "let's go fishing." They would get up, and go either to the state of Wisconsin or Michigan. This was a vacation to them after working all week long. They looked forward to spending quality time doing what they both enjoyed doing.

After several of years had gone by, Euphemia began talking to Wealthy about getting married. He did not give an answer right away, but Wealthy would not marry her until he was sure that he loved her. Wealthy began to pray to God about the situation because he wanted to be sure that Euphemia was the woman he should marry. One Saturday morning, the Lord woke Wealthy up saying, "this is it" and he touched Euphemia. She responded, "what?" "What you been asking me about, we can do it now," he explained. She said, "What get married?" Wealthy replied, "yes." Euphemia was very excited about getting married to him. So, they put on some casual clothes, and went to get their blood test. They didn't wear formal attire because the snow was about 1 foot deep. After getting their blood test done, they went to the City Hall and got married the same day, January 20, 1962. After their marriage ceremony, they went to a nearby store called Murray Majors and bought $300 worth of fishing gear. They were preparing to go fishing in the Spring.

Euphemia and Wealthy L. Mobley Sr.

Wealthy and Euphemia's love and Christianity continued to grow stronger. Euphemia was a Seven-day Adventist. While, Wealthy was in the Baptist Church. She soon converted over to the Baptist church to serve the Lord with her husband at Original Mount Pleasant Missionary Baptist Church. She served as an Usher for over 17 years there. Later both Wealthy and Euphemia went to the Chicago Baptist Institute. Wealthy graduated from there with a Bachelor of Theology degree, and Euphemia got a certificate of Christian Education. She taught Sunday School for 40 years. Every church that they joined, she would teach Sunday School.

During the course of their marriage, they went on 14 cruises. A couple of cruises they went to were the Bahamas and Aruba. These islands were very memorable for their climates. A hurricane would hit near the Bahamas every two years. They enjoyed Aruba the most, because this country, rarely had any storms. For this reason, they were wondering if they could live in that kind of climate all the time. So, they went there twice. They went to the Bahamas a few times with Wealthy's brother Eugene Jr. and his wife Mamie Till Mobley whom both were activists. All day long they had picnics, listened to music and danced. The two couples enjoyed vacationing in the Caribbean together.

Wealthy and Eugene Jr. were very close. He explained that Eugene Jr., "was born March 26, 1923. People thought he was the oldest because he was outspoken." Their careers were most compatible. Both Wealthy and Eugene Jr. worked in the automobile industry. Wealthy retired from Ford Motor Company in 1980 and Eugene Jr. retired from Hanley Dawson Cadillac in 1987. And Euphemia and Mamie both worked as educators. Euphemia worked in the Christian Educational Department with the youth and Mamie taught elementary students in the Chicago Public Schools. Teaching children is commendable, with the goal of them becoming better human beings both academically and spiritually.

Life Struggles

Euphemia and Wealthy's main struggles during their marriage were when they became chronically ill. Euphemia had emphysema and needed oxygen twenty-four hours, seven days a week. This slowed her down from traveling and cooking indefinitely. He adds, "I miss her cooking." But Wealthy picked up the slack and began cooking for his wife as much as he could. He was very attentive to his wife's every need. He explains that he now has colon cancer. These illnesses occurred when they were in their late 80's and early 90's. Up until their health failed them, they were still traveling and enjoying life.

Over fifty years later, Euphemia and Wealthy L. Mobley Sr. were still married. The forces that kept their marriage together were having love and respect for one another. He confirms, "I love her and gonna be right there with her, till death do us part. That's what's going to do it." These words he spoke with a spark of love for her in his eyes.

Racism Unveiled

"The Lord is my light and my salvation; whom shall I fear? The Lord is the strength of my life; of whom shall I be afraid?" (Psalm27:1)

Euphemia and her sister-in-law, Eugene Jr's wife, Mamie were able to identify with one another, the pain of losing a child is indescribable. Euphemia's son Donald was killed in an automobile crash. In 1955, Mamie's only biological child, 14 year old Emmett Till, was forced from the home of his great-uncle in Money, Mississippi by Roy Bryant and J. W. Milam. He was later found dead in the Tallahatchie River with a gin fan tied around his neck, holding his lifeless body down. Also, he had been severely mangled beyond recognition, and shot in the head. His young life was taken for allegedly coming on to Carolyn Bryant, a white woman, and wife to Roy Bryant.

Reality is, lynching was certainly nothing new in Mississippi within the regions of the Delta. Very little was done about it, if it was a black person. Most black people feared what might happen to either themselves or their family. So, they were not going to say anything. However, fear can shape a person's character despite their race. Causing one to be afraid of whatever could or would cause pain and threaten their state of being. It takes courage to speak out against injustice and inequality. The story of Emmett Till has been told and written about many of times. The kill of Emmett raises awareness that systemic racism still exists; it has been this way for black people since the United States of America was founded on July 4, 1776.

Unlike any other lynching in the south, Emmett Till's death sent a strong hurricane throughout the nation. The violent wind sent waves, piercing the hearts of both young and old people. The loud thunder and lightning zoomed in on racism like never before. The rain from it, left a lasting effect, causing a nation to see how senseless, hateful, and cruel racism is. This all happened because Mamie, decided to have an open-casket, and a publicized visitation of his maimed and brutally tortured body for thousands of people to see, at the A. A. Rayner Funeral Home of Chicago. This is what galvanized the nation and moved the Civil Rights Movement to a different level. The purpose of this was to unveil to the world what they had done to her son because of racism. This horrific crime against Emmett Till was seen on television, various news stations, newspapers and magazines. Eyes were opened, and ears heard Mamie's cry for justice. This catalyzed Mississippi to move forward with a trial.

During the trial, Mamie was a resident of Chicago. So, throughout the trial for Emmett Till, Wealthy claims, "Mamie stayed with Dr. Howard in Mound Bayou." Dr. Theodore Roosevelt Mason Howard was a Doctor and a Civil Rights Activist. Mound Bayou was a city where accomplished black people lived and owned their own homes, although this city was located in the region of the Mississippi Delta. Wealthy commented, "He was so powerful there." Out of all that was done to share with the world about this heinous crime, the accused murderers, Roy Bryant and J.W. Milam were acquitted by an all-white jury. After the trial, Wealthy mentioned that Dr. Howard moved to Chicago because "they wanted to kill him."

Mamie was a courageous and resilient woman. The manner in which her son was killed alone was overwhelming and could induce thoughts of either suicide or a state of depression. It's obvious that she did not allow these thoughts to overtake her. Instead, she used the strength that she had, to continue the fight for justice for her son. This gave people all over the country the will to confront injustice fearlessly, and unapologetically.

Civil Rights Activist Eugene Mobley Jr. (Gene) passed away on March 18, 2000, and Mamie Till-Mobley expired on January 6, 2003.

Euphemia and Eugene Mobley Jr.

Euphemia and Mamie Till-Mobley

CHRISTIAN WALK OF FAITH

"And Samuel said, 'Hath the Lord as great delight in obeying the voice of the Lord? Behold, to obey is better than sacrifice, and to hearken than the fat of rams." (1 Samuel 15:22)

Of course, Wealthy was religious. He was raised up going to church with both his mother and grandmother. He didn't know any other way.

It was on a sunny Friday evening in the month of May, in 1933, after the death of his mother that the Lord saved Wealthy. He went to a little church sitting out in the woods with his grandmother. At this church they were having a revival. Before he went into the church, he heard how the people in the church were praising and worshipping God. While listening, an unusual feeling came over him. This feeling he had never felt before. After that, with tears rolling down his face, he began to pray saying, "Lord, I don't know what this is, but whatever it is, save me and let me know that I'm saved." After he prayed, there was a light shining all around him. He knew it wasn't the sun because the sun had gone down. It was now dark. So, he took off running toward the church saying, "I got it." When he got to the door of the church, it opened, his grandmother said, "he got it, that boy got it," and the people in the church started to do more shouting. There was a change in his life, but he had to grow.

At the age of thirteen, he and relatives established a quintet group in Mississippi called The Cousin Five. This group included: Wealthy, his two brothers Vernon Brown, and Eugene and his two cousins, Oscar and David Brown. Their singing abilities were so good that their parents began taking them to different places to perform. After they moved to Chicago in 1935, they joined a church called Pleasant Green on the 2900 block of Cottage Grove, where Reverend Newton was the Pastor. This was a storefront church. Wealthy got baptized. The Cousin Five were still together during this time. They continued to sing, but not as much, for the "bright lights and girls," Wealthy points out. However, when Wealthy was inducted into the army, they all went their separate ways. Wealthy still continued to sing while in the army. He began singing with a group called Special Service. Wealthy did not neglect the gift within him.

Spiritual Obedience

One Friday evening, after leaving work from the Ford Motor Company, Wealthy and a friend decided to go and have a drink at a tavern called Ms. Mack. He and his friend would go there every Friday after work and get themselves a half pint of Cognac. They sat down and ordered their usual but as the bartender began pouring Wealthy's drink into a glass, the Spirit spoke to him saying, "what are you doing in here." Wealthy got up from the bar, and the bartender said, "what's the matter, didn't I pour you the right thang?" Wealthy replied saying, "yeah." So, he sat back down, and the Spirit said, "get out of here." Sweat came pouring down his face. His friend said, "hey Moe, what's up?" Wealthy said, "I don't know, but I'm getting out of here." When he got home, his wife was cleaning. She said, "what's the matter?" Wealthy didn't respond to her at that moment. He just stayed in the house, "praying, repenting, and thanking the Lord," Wealthy explained. He began to reminisce his experience with the Lord when he had first gotten saved. A revelation unfolded, he implies, "once you've been saved, he's going to hold you; hey! You ain't going no further." After that night, Wealthy never had another drink of alcohol. He then went back to church and things started falling in their proper perspective. *"While it is said, To day if ye will hear his voice, harden not your hearts, as in the provocation."* (Hebrew 3:15)

In the early 1960's, Wealthy joined the Original Mount Pleasant Missionary Baptist Church under the late Reverend Billy Kyles, where his grandmother Mary Smith and a host of other relatives were members. After becoming a member of the church, he joined the choir. His grandmother was the mother of the church and she also sang in the choir. She was a very spiritual woman. One morning, she was cooking in her home and she got happy. "She was cooking biscuits, I could smell them," said Wealthy. All of a sudden, she said, "Alleluia, thank you, Jesus." When she did that, she just threw the whole pan. The biscuits went everywhere. He wasn't worried about it, he looked at her and she was shouting. Wealthy just went and started picking up the biscuits. He remembered her being an active member of a church since he was a child. She was both a father and a mother to Wealthy. She made her transition in mid 1962.

In 1962, Wealthy was elected as the Choir President for 7 years at Original Mount Pleasant under the leadership of Reverend Jelks. Wealthy then became active in Sunday School. H.R. Jelks saw how faithful he and his wife were to the church, he approved a Christian Education Scholarship for them to attend the Chicago Baptist Institute of Chicago. He was excited about going back to school. He no longer had to worry about being taken out of school to satisfy government policies. Later, Pastor Jelks died, then Reverend Royce D. Cornelius became pastor in 1970.

After Rev. Cornelius became pastor at Original Mount Pleasant, he saw the divine leadership in Wealthy. Within that same year, the pastor ordained Wealthy as a Deacon while he was still attending school. He then was promoted to General Superintendent of the Sunday School and the Bus ministry. He and his wife would pick up adults and children from their homes so they could attend Sunday School.

In 1975, Wealthy became aware of his spiritual purpose. He began to recollect about how the Lord had been protecting and preserving him so he could be used of Him. Wealthy believes that God had protected him all while in the army. He accepted his spiritual call to the ministry and Rev. Cornelius ordained him and made him the Youth Pastor.

Wealthy Graduated From The Chicago Bible Institute

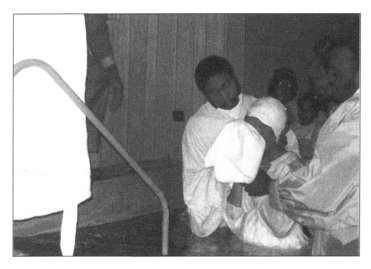

Rev. Mobley Baptizing a Parishioner

In February 1978, Wealthy was elected as Pastor at the Cathedral of Love Missionary Baptist Church. During that time, he was still employed with the Ford Motor Company. It was very unusual to Wealthy how he became a candidate to pastor this church. In October 1977, a member of Original Mount Pleasant asked if he would do an eulogy for a members' brother at Cathedral of Love. He went there, did the eulogy, and never wondered about the pastor's absence. Wealthy commented "the Spirit wouldn't let me do that." A few months later, someone from Cathedral of Love called him and explained that they were without a pastor, and that they were considering him. This came as a surprise to Wealthy because he was content in serving in Original Mount Pleasant.

He later accepted the role of pastor at the Cathedral of Love. There were many members including ministers that followed him from Original Mount Pleasant. A couple to follow were Jacqueline Douglas and Lennie Ramsey. Wealthy pastored there for almost 11 years. Wealthy acknowledges that, "Half of the 11 years at Cathedral of Love was beautiful." He enjoyed going on different trips with the church. He remembered going to Pittsburgh, Philadelphia and Houston with the Bible Training Union

Christian Education department throughout the years. However, he adds, "things started to happen." The deacons requested that he resign from his job and that the church would take care of him. Wealthy thought about it. He only had to work between 3 to 4 years before being eligible to retire. He began to pray about the situation. The Spirit said, " no you don't," Wealthy implied. So, he obeyed the Spirit. That way he could get his retirement and didn't have to preach appeasement.

Euphemia and Rev. Wealthy L. Mobley Sr.
at Cathedral of Love

Now, after Wealthy did retire, he recalls seeing "things going on concerning the church that wasn't right." He began speaking out against it whether it be for the natural or spiritual betterment of the church. The deacons were not pleased with this. So, one of the deacons said to him, "all we want you to do is preach, we'll take care of the church." Wealthy replied saying, "but you sent for a pastor, you didn't send for somebody to preach." When he would go away, the deacons would have meetings about his pastoring abilities. Wealthy knew the plot against him. But he did not retaliate against them. "That's what the spirit of God will do for you," he commented.

So, the 1st Sunday in November 1988, before Wealthy preached, the Spirit took him all over the church. Then the Spirit led him to the pulpit, and said, "look, what do you see?" He responded, "nothing." The Spirit then said, "that's right, get going." That day Wealthy resigned from being Pastor at the Cathedral of Love.

Who Can Build a House for God?

"And I say also unto thee, That thou art Peter, and upon this rock I will build my church; and the gates of hell shall not prevail against it." (Matthew 16:18)

When Wealthy resigned from being Pastor at Cathedral of Love, over 100 people followed him from there. Being the leader that he is, he was compelled by the Lord to find a place of worship for these people. So, the 2nd Sunday in November, 1988, he and the parishioners met at the Burton Funeral Home of Chicago to have service. It was then when The Gospel Truth Missionary Baptist Church was born. They were so happy that the Burton Funeral Home opened their doors to them. But it didn't have the seating capacity for the membership.

Later, Wealthy spoke to Eugene Jr. and his sister-in-law Mamie Till-Mobley about the dilemma they were in. In response to the churches' dilemma, Mamie contacted her friend Mrs. Lorenza Brown-Porter and explained the churches situation. She in turn contacted her employer, the Gatling Chapel Inc. located in Chicago. Then Wealthy and his brother Eugene Jr. met with Marquerite and Lafayette Gatling Sr., and they came to an agreement for them to have services on their premises rent free, enabling the church to save money.

The Gospel Truth as a whole, continued services in Gatling Chapel for six years. Throughout these years, some members began to complain about having their worship services in the funeral home. Though some of the members continued to complain, Wealthy continued to pray, and began to seek other churches that they could have service. Finally, they arranged to have worship services in other churches located in Chicago. Some of the names are as follows: The Late Rev. Eugene Gibson of Mission of Faith M.B. Church, Pastor Rainey of Christian Fellowship Church, Pastor Q. Z. Gardner of New Macedonia M. B. Church, and Pastor Waddell of Paxton Avenue Church. Though Wealthy did have worship services in various places, he did not lose focus of the vision for The Gospel Truth to someday have their own edifice.

Later, Wealthy and the church board began to search for a place of their own to have worship service. They did not find nothing to their expectations. Then it was propositioned that they should build a church. This proposition was taken under consideration, and the church began to raise funds for this purpose. The church as a whole, raised over $97,000 by coming together on one accord, working for one common goal. After diligently searching for land to build on. They finally found a commercial lot in the 100th block of Halsted Street. The property was listed over $127,000, but The Gospel Truth purchased it at $97,500.

It was February 26, 1995 when The Gospel Truth broke ground for their new church. March 6, 1995, they began to build. Through prayer, dedication, and working on one accord, the church was built from the ground up in only ninety days. Some members expressed displeasure in the church being built too fast. Really, it was an act of faith.

After the church was built, the Lord added to the church. There were 19 ministers to join the church under the leadership of Rev. Mobley. He still remained humble. He understood what it took to spiritually build a house for God, the same measures are needed to maintain it. The parishioners at The Gospel Truth continued to work hard. Both the late

Minister David Word and John McNeal, former members of The Gospel Truth, were known for doing fundraisers for the church. They were very dedicated and loved the church. Min. David Word directed plays, and John McNeal enjoyed presenting concerts. One concert that John presented was on the 1991 fellowship cruise at Nassau, Bahamas. He and the late Albertina Walker did a duet and had the church on their feet praising God. Being that the fellowship cruise fundraiser was a success, it was continued until 2002. Though Albertina Walker was a very successful gospel singer, she would periodically come to The Gospel Truth to enjoy the worship service. But she would render a song just for the asking. Also, Reverend Keith B. Hayes Sr. directed many successful fundraisers for the church.

Even now, over 20 years later, Wealthy is still humble, and thankful to God for allowing him to be the founder and pastor of The Gospel Truth Missionary Baptist Church. Also, in November 2008, he considers it a blessing to see the church paid in full.

Original Mount Pleasant Missionary Baptist Church

Cathedral of Love Missionary Baptist Church

The Gospel Truth Missionary Baptist Church

A Shepard's Heart

"As for me, I have not hastened from being a pastor to follow thee: neither have I desired the woeful day; thou knowest: that which came out of my lips was right before thee." (Jeremiah 17:16)

Reverend Dr. Royce D. Cornelius is the Pastor of Christ Church of Chicago, Illinois. Also, he is the pastor of Rev. Mobley. They came to know one another in 1965. Rev. Cornelius was a young evangelist at the time. He was assigned to preach every 2nd and 4th Sunday of each month at the Original Mount Pleasant Missionary Baptist Church where Rev. Mobley was a member.

Rev. Cornelius is thankful to God for Rev. Mobley being born under his ministry. He was a choir member and the Lord led him to ordain him as a deacon. From there, he rose in the ranks like he did in the army. He was promoted to General Superintendent of Sunday School and the Bus Ministry. Later, Rev. Cornelius ordained him as a minister. He was then appointed as the Youth Pastor. After Rev. Mobley received his own right to becoming a pastor, he still honors and loves Rev. Cornelius in reflection of all they shared.

There are characteristics and qualities of a pastor that Rev. Cornelius could identify and appreciate about Rev. Mobley. These characteristics are dedication to ministry, humility and unfailing love for people.

Rev. Mobley has a strong dedication to ministry, and the study of the bible. He's one of the few preachers that Rev. Cornelius has known who has read God's word daily and has read the bible many times in its entirety.

Also, he has a humility that's rare. He's neither an arrogant nor prevailing pastor. But, he is one who has a humble spirit, and "often he would take 'no' for the sake of peace, believing that the power of the words that he dispenses, will rectify and ratify any problems that might arise in his ministry." For example, Cathedral of Love Missionary Baptist Church selected him to be their pastor. After getting there, he found that he was in an oppressed situation, when he was not allowed to neither exercise his gift nor his mission. The officials of the church rose tough on him. Most ministers would have just resigned and gone on their way to a place where they could be more free. But not Rev. Mobley, he stayed there under those circumstances, and eventually, won those people over to him by his spirit of humility. They were overwhelmed that he was such a gentleman. Yet, a man with the power to have fought back, but he refused to do so. This alone, proved an unfailing love for the people that he was assigned to pastor. "I think that those things are not just for him, but for anyone who aspires to be a pastor," said Rev. Cornelius.

Rev. Mobley had been an example as well as a friend to Rev. Cornelius in many ways saying, "that cause me to task everyday as I analyze myself, and see my short comings as I see myself in comparison to him." Additionally, he explains that "Mobley gives me courage. He is a family man and husband of the first latitude. For he has been married almost 60 years to the same woman. She's in her 90s', and she needs to have constant attendance. But, he is at her beck and call. Rev. Mobley presents a love for her, that is incomparable. That helps me and it gives me a great role model. "

Rev. Dr. Edgar Woodall is the pastor at Friendship Missionary Baptist Church of Anderson, Indiana. He came to know Rev. Mobley about 20 years ago when he came to do a revival. He and the late Pastor J.C. Galmore are cousins. "The two churches have been fellowshipping since the revival," said Rev. Woodall.

He's able to appreciate how knowledgeable Rev. Mobley is in the scriptures, and how he is such a kind Christian person. "When we fellowship together, I get to experience that closeness that we have. Being able to converse with him one on one." His ability to teach the word of God is like a magnet. Through which people are drawn to him because of his charisma. Rev. Woodall explains, "he has an aura around him that draws people."

More importantly, Rev. Mobley is one who has helped many to be children of God. Also, teaching a young man how to be a man. Whom would be: honored and reverenced in God's church, in the city, the nation, and the world.

Rev. Edgar Woodall

Rev. Royce D. Cornelius

Evangelist Aubreydella Gordon-Hay is a former member of The Gospel Truth Missionary Baptist Church. She came to know Rev. Mobley by Mr. and Mrs. Gatling, of the Gatling Funeral Home Inc.

While being a member under the teaching of Rev. Mobley, Evg. Gordon-Hay grew spiritually. She said she learned to, "trust in the Lord with all your heart; lean not to your own understanding."

One thing Evg. Gordon-Hay wants the world to know is that Rev. Mobley constantly showed her love at all times.

Minister Charles Ivory met Rev. Mobley over a decade ago. He came to The Gospel Truth Missionary Baptist Church to attend a revival.

The Rev. Campbell of the Church of God in Christ did not show-up to do the revival, so Rev. Mobley put Min. Ivory up to bring the message. So, Min. Ivory had been coming to the church ever since.

Min. Ivory makes oil that grow the hair. He thanks God for Rev. Mobley. He found him to be very nice in encouraging him to do bigger and better things, and allowing him to sell his products at the church. He likes the fact that, spiritually so, Rev. Mobley preaches that actions speaks louder than words.

Most of all, he thanks God for the fact that Rev. Mobley loves his family, and his church by imparting the word of God on a consistent basis. Min. Ivory said, "A man is only as strong as his lifestyle." Preachers and teachers must be an example to the believers. He has found Rev. Mobley to be an example for men to provide for their families. Min. Ivory said, "He impresses me tremendously." "*Let no man despise thy youth; but be thou an example of the believers, in word, in conversation, in charity, in spirit, in faith, in purity.*" (1 Timothy 4:12)

Minister Spunny Thomas came to know Rev. Mobley in 1978 when he came to eulogize a member of Cathedral of Love in 1978. He is the person who advised their Pulpit Committee to contact Mobley for consideration of becoming the pastor of their church. Mobley came over a couple of times to preach and teach the word of God. They found that he was full of the Spirit and wisdom. They felt he was the person for the job. So, it wasn't long before they made him the pastor.

Min. Thomas watched Rev. Mobley pastor down through the years, and found him to be a honest man. He has experienced him having patience to counsel him and others, saving them embarrassment of error in the public eye. Min. Thomas believes that Mobley lives the kind of life, that he can go anywhere without being ashamed.

Parental Wisdom

Rev. Mobley emphasizes that, "Being a father, I wanted to be the best for my children. God blessed me to be able to provide for them, and to see them grow up in the Lord. Being that example, not just telling them, but let them see it in me. I baptized every one of them, led by example. I didn't tell them, I took them to church, ball games, and fishing. They want to see you. Now, even more so, it has magnified into something beautiful. Not only are they my children, they are my friends. I can lay in my bed now and say, thank you Lord. Cause he had done it for me."

Also, He considers it a blessing to have three children, Phyllis Mobley-Johnson, Deacon Wealthy L. Mobley Jr., and Reverend Vanessa Ervin. "*Train up a child in the way*

he should go: and when he is old, he will not depart from it."
(Proverbs 22:6)

Memories

Phyllis Mobley-Johnson

Her earliest memories of her father were moments spent sitting in the car and going with him to make deliveries.

Now that Phyllis is grown, enriched with Gods' words, it gives her great pleasure being in church with him and seeing him be loved by so many people.

Also, Phyllis mentions, "I admire the strength, determination, the power in the word that God has given him. This man has really, he still, encourages me all the time. And, I just respect him. I thank Jehovah for him."

Deacon Wealthy L. Mobley Jr.

In 1955, Dea. Mobley Jr. remembered his father buying a car. He loved going for car rides in it with his father. Also, as a child, he wished that he could have spent more time with him.

Looking back over his life as a man of God, he knows his father did the best he could. Now Dea. Mobley Jr. emphasizes, "he has become my best friend and mentor."

Also, he takes special pleasure in his spiritual blessings and teachings that his father shared with him. Which he believes now, are the basics of his Christian life.

Reverend Vanessa Ervin

As a little girl, Rev. Ervin remembered she and her father going to McDonald's. She would get a cheeseburger, fries and an orange drink. She reveals, "Still to this day, 58 years later, my favorite meal at McDonald's is this meal."

Also, as a child, Rev. Ervin grew up in church. She loved to hear her father sing. Vanessa comments, "He had such a beautiful voice." Later as an adult, she was called into ministry, and her father licensed and ordained her as a minister.

Now as an ordained minister, she is amazed and encouraged by his tremendous resilience to preach the word of God at age 92. Rev. Ervin points out that, "He loves to study, he loves to teach. If he could do that 24/7 he would."

90TH YEAR BIRTHDAY CELEBRATION

"So teach us to number our days, that we may apply our hearts unto wisdom." (Psalm 90:12)

Dear Reverend Mobley:

We are pleased to join your family and friends in wishing you all the best on your birthday.

You have witnessed great milestones in our Nation's history, and your generation has shown the courage to persevere through moments of uncertainty and challenge. Your story is an important part of the American narrative, and we hope you will look back with joy and pride on the many contributions and memories made over the course of your life.

As you celebrate this special occasion, we wish you health and happiness in the years ahead.

Sincerely,

Michelle Obama

A letter from the First Lady Michelle, and President Barack Obama

Rev. Mobley celebrating his 9oth Year Birthday

Euphemia and Rev. Wealth L. Mobley Sr.

Felicia and Rev. Keith B. Hayes Sr.

The Gospel Truth Church Parishioners and Friends

Mrs. Lorenza Brown-Porter

Rev. Mobley and Wealthy L. Mobley Jr.

Rev. Mobley and Phyllis Mobley-Johnson

Friends From the ACLC

Rev. Mobley and Deacon Clint Towers

Unforgettable Stains

"Surely he shall not be moved forever: the righteous shall be in everlasting remembrance." (Psalm 112:6)

Reverend Mobley, being the humble and kind man that he is did not believe in living a life of regret. So, he trusted in God to lead and guide him into his destiny. Rev. Mobley believes that his past and present life experiences prepared him for the role of a pastor.

His childhood chores were hard domestic labor, but it made him strong both naturally and spiritually. Living in the Mississippi Delta during the Jim Crow Era prepared him for a segregated US Army.

In the US Army he rose in the ranks to Staff Sergeant. He oversaw about 40 black soldiers, both young and old. This taught him to lead by example. Additionally, all the life-threatening situations he escaped in the US Army could have been his end. But, he was never seriously injured. God brought him out safely.

About thirty years after being honorably discharged from the US Army as a Staff Sergeant and WWII Veteran, he obtained a bachelors' degree in Theology. He accepted his calling into ministry. Later, he received a honorary doctorates degree.

This man with a vision, became the founder and pastor of The Gospel Truth Missionary Baptist Church. Overseeing hundreds of people locally. He welcomed the homeless to sit in on Sunday's services and fed them when they were hungry.

Euphemia and Rev. Dr. Wealthy L. Mobley Sr.
of The Gospel Truth Missionary Baptist Church

Rev. Dr. Wealthy L. Mobley Sr.'s name can be found:

The founder and pastor of The Gospel Truth Missionary Baptist Church.

From 101st to Highway I-57 on West 99th Street. Halsted Street was renamed Rev. Dr. Wealthy L. Mobley Street

Echoing his voice to *'Mountain Top Meditations'* radio broadcast with his pastor and friend, Rev. Dr. Royce D. Cornelius.

In the 2000-2001 edition of 'Who's Who in America" in the Library of Congress.

In 2007, The Gospel Truth Missionary Baptist Church choir released a CD entitled *Give Me the Gospel Truth*.

In 2010, HISTORY OF THE GOSPEL TRUTH MISSIONARY BAPTIST CHURCH book written by the late Evangelist Joyce Ann Betts

Rev. Dr. Wealthy L. Mobley Sr., Founder and Pastor of The Gospel Truth Missionary Baptist Church

Rev. Mobley's race had been run. His mission for God, completed. After his soulmate, Euphemia Haynes-Mobley died April 22, 2013. Less than a month later, he expired May 17, 2013.

Though his life has come to an end, Rev. Dr. Wealthy L. Mobley Sr's legacy yet remains. He had a habit of encouraging his parishioners to obey God with these words,

"GOD WILL NOT LET FAITHFULNESS GO UNREWARDED"

CPSIA information can be obtained
at www.ICGtesting.com
Printed in the USA
LVHW072124121021
700249LV00019B/533